NOV 1 9 2020

CARDBOARD CASTLE CHALLENGE!

Sue Gagliardi

DiscoverRoo
An Imprint of Pop!
popbooksonline.com

abdobooks.com

Published by Pop!, a division of ABDO, PO Box 398166, Minneapolis, Minnesota 55439. Copyright © 2021 by POP, LLC. International copyrights reserved in all countries. No part of this book may be reproduced in any form without written permission from the publisher. Pop!™ is a trademark and logo of POP, LLC.

Printed in the United States of America, North Mankato, Minnesota.

052020
092020

Cover Photos: Shutterstock Images, top left, top right, bottom
Interior Photos: Shutterstock Images, 1 (top left), 1 (top right), 1 (bottom), 9, 15, 21; iStockphoto, 4–5, 6, 7, 8, 11, 12, 13, 14, 17, 22 (boxes), 22 (tubes), 22 (scissors), 23, 25, 26, 28, 30, 31; Dorling Kindersley ltd/Alamy, 18; MediaWorldImages/Alamy, 19; Craig Russell/Alamy, 20; Malcolm Fairman/Alamy, 27; Peter Byrne/PA Images/Alamy, 29

Editor: Meg Gaertner
Series Designer: Jake Slavik

Library of Congress Control Number: 2019954981
Publisher's Cataloging-in-Publication Data

Names: Gagliardi, Sue, author.

Title: Cardboard castle challenge! / by Sue Gagliardi

Description: Minneapolis, Minnesota : POP!, 2021 | Series: Makerspace cardboard challenge! | Includes online resources and index.

Identifiers: ISBN 9781532167911 (lib. bdg.) | ISBN 9781644944516 (pbk.) | ISBN 9781532169014 (ebook)

Subjects: LCSH: Cardboard art--Juvenile literature. | Crafts (Handicrafts)--Juvenile literature. | Creative thinking in children--Juvenile literature. | Maker spaces--Juvenile literature.

Classification: DDC 745.54--dc23

WELCOME TO
DiscoverRoo!

Pop open this book and you'll find QR codes loaded with information, so you can learn even more!

Scan this code* and others like it while you read, or visit the website below to make this book pop!

popbooksonline.com/castle-challenge

*Scanning QR codes requires a web-enabled smart device with a QR code reader app and a camera.

TABLE OF CONTENTS

CHAPTER 1
SAFETY AND SHELTER

Castles are large, strong buildings. They give people safety and shelter. Castles have thick, high walls. They have tall towers. These structures can stand up

The walled medieval city of Carcassonne in France includes a castle.

against enemy attacks. Castles also serve as homes for the **nobility**.

WATCH A VIDEO HERE!

Many castles were built on hills.

This gave people inside a clear view

of the nearby land. They could see

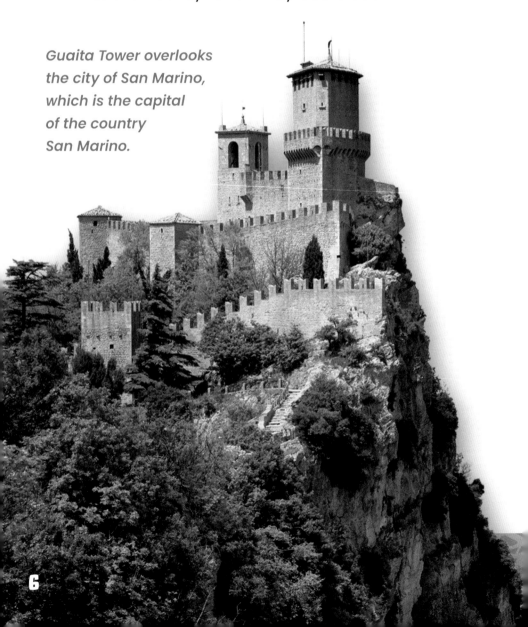

*Guaita Tower overlooks
the city of San Marino,
which is the capital
of the country
San Marino.*

Hohenzollern Castle in Germany has been rebuilt many times over the centuries.

approaching enemies. People often built villages near castles.

THINK ABOUT IT

Why do you think people built villages near castles?

Many moats are filled with water.

Castles were often surrounded

by **moats**. These ditches made it

hard for enemies to reach the castle.

People inside used **drawbridges** to control who could enter.

CASTLE NAMES

Castles can have different names depending on their purposes. Castles built mainly for protection are called fortresses. They may also be called forts or strongholds. People built these castles in key places. The places were easy to guard. Castles built mainly as homes may be called manors or palaces. In France, these castles are called *chateaus*.

People could cut off entry by raising the drawbridge from inside the castle.

CHAPTER 2
INSIDE A CASTLE

People first built castles out of wood.

Then people began using stone. This

stronger material gave more protection.

Curtain walls surrounded the entire

castle. Many castles had inner courtyards

LEARN MORE HERE!

Spiš Castle is one of the largest castles in Central Europe. It was built in the 1100s.

called baileys. Baileys gave people a

place to get fresh air and light. People

could go outside and still be protected by

the curtain walls.

Towers rise high from the Palace of the Grand Master of the Knights of Rhodes in Greece.

People designed castles to be easily

guarded. High towers rose above the

walls. The towers provided safe **lookouts**

THINK ABOUT IT

Why do you think fighters in the castle would need to shoot arrows? Why wouldn't they just stay safe inside the castle?

for defenders. The walls often had small holes. Fighters could shoot arrows out through the holes.

Arrow slits were thin, vertical gaps in a wall or tower.

arrow slit

Castles often had one large tower called a keep. It would usually be at the center of the castle. **Nobility** lived in the keep. The keep was also a place to stay safe. If enemy fighters managed to enter the castle, defenders could retreat to the keep for safety.

Some castles still stand after hundreds of years.

PARTS OF A CASTLE

tower

drawbridge

keep

moat

bailey

curtain wall

Raglan Castle in Wales has a dry moat inside the castle. A drawbridge over the moat leads into the keep.

CHAPTER 3
CASTLE CHALLENGE

People have been building castles for

hundreds of years. Challenge yourself

to build a castle out of cardboard. Real

castles have many parts. They can have

COMPLETE AN ACTIVITY HERE!

Many castles have stairs and places for people to stand along the curtain walls.

curtain walls, towers, keeps, and baileys.

What parts will your castle have?

Castle builders in the past used mortar to hold stones together. Mortar is a thick, sticky paste. They made the mortar out of **lime**, soil, and water.

You could connect parts of your castle by cutting slits in the cardboard.

The makers of this cardboard castle used lots of tape to hold the pieces together.

What materials could you use to hold your castle together? Which materials would be the strongest?

A model is a small version of something. This model is of Hogwarts Castle from the Harry Potter movies.

Consider drawing your castle

first. Sketch a design on paper. Then,

build a small model. See if your

design works. After that, try building a

human-sized castle.

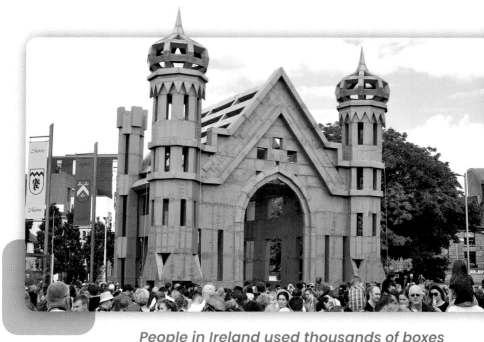

People in Ireland used thousands of boxes to build this cardboard castle in 2017.

THINK ABOUT IT

Why might people make models of objects before building the life-size versions?

SUPPLY LIST

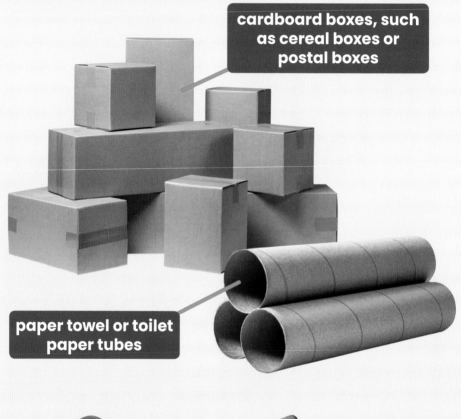

cardboard boxes, such as cereal boxes or postal boxes

paper towel or toilet paper tubes

scissors

ruler   tape or glue   paper and pencil

paint and paintbrushes   string or yarn

construction paper   crayons or markers

CHAPTER 4
IMPROVING YOUR DESIGN

Castles protected people from enemy attacks. Buildings can guard people from other forces too. For example, buildings need to stay standing in strong winds. How could you add weight to your castle

LEARN MORE HERE!

Some castles served mostly as people's homes. How could you decorate your castle? How could you make it somewhere nice to live?

or attach your castle to the ground? Use

a fan to test your design.

A castle's thick walls kept it standing tall so the people inside stayed safe.

Castles often had **drawbridges**

and **moats**. People used thick chains

to raise and lower the drawbridges.

What materials could you use to make a

Not all moats were filled with water. Dry moats were still hard to cross without a drawbridge.

These children used string to make their drawbridge. The string runs from the end of the drawbridge to the top of the castle wall.

working drawbridge? What materials

could you use for a moat?

Fighters shot arrows from the castle walls and towers.

Castles helped people guard themselves. For example, people could use tall towers as **lookouts**. They could see approaching enemies. What could you use to support taller towers in your castle? What else could you add to your castle to help people defend it?

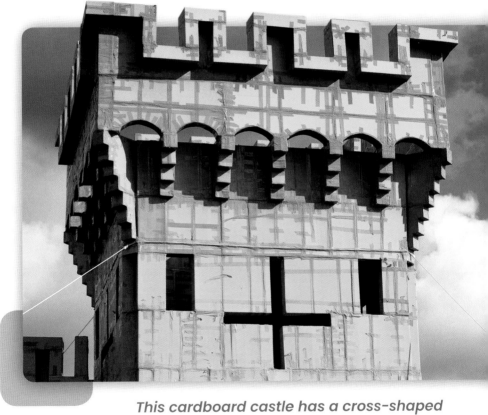

This cardboard castle has a cross-shaped arrow slit in its tower.

MAKING CONNECTIONS

TEXT-TO-SELF

Would you want to live in a castle? Why or why not?

TEXT-TO-TEXT

Have you read other books about using recycled materials to make something new? Which things would you like trying to make?

TEXT-TO-WORLD

The Cardboard Challenge is a way to create something new using recycled materials. How does your community recycle? How does recycling benefit your community?

GLOSSARY

curtain wall – the outer wall of a castle that protects the inner courtyard and keep.

drawbridge – a bridge that can be raised up or let down.

lime – a white substance made by heating limestone and used in building.

lookout – a high place from which people can easily view the surrounding land.

moat – a ditch that surrounds a castle and keeps intruders from entering.

nobility – a social class of high-ranking people.

INDEX

ONLINE RESOURCES

popbooksonline.com

Scan this code* and others like it while you read, or visit the website below to make this book pop!

popbooksonline.com/castle-challenge

*Scanning QR codes requires a web-enabled smart device with a QR code reader app and a camera.